NATIONAL GEOGRA
School Pu

Soaring with Science

PATHFINDER EDITION

By Susan Halko

CONTENTS

Soarin

American ski jumper Lindsey Van waits for her turn at the top of the hill. There's the green light. Go! She pushes off of the bar. She's gaining speed. She reaches the jump and launches into the air. Look at her form. She's really catching air! Now she glides down for the landing. Her skis gracefully touch down. She bends her knees and gradually skis to a stop. What a sensational jump! Believe it or not, the laws of motion are at work during a jump like this. How? What do they have to do with ski jumping? Let's find out.

The Newton Connection

On February 20, 2009, Lindsey Van won the first-ever gold medal in Women's Ski Jumping at the World Championships.

Lindsey used her athletic ability to make the jump, but the laws of motion were also involved. You see, famous scientist Sir Isaac Newton figured out rules for how things move. He described his rules as the three laws of motion.

Let's look at Lindsey's jump. From the moment she pushes off the top of the hill until she skis to a stop at the bottom, Newton's laws of motion play a key role.

Major Motion. A little science helps ski jumpers go a long way.

with Science

By Susan Halko

Steps of a Ski Jump

1. In-run

2. Take off

3. Flight

Forces at Work

Newton's first law says that to move an object at rest, a **force** must get the object going. A force is a push or pull that makes something move. Lindsey uses force to push off the bar. That force makes her move.

As she comes down the slide, Lindsey needs to go as fast as possible. She knows that forces will work with her and against her. The force of gravity will help her. It pulls her down the hill, helping her move faster.

The force of **friction**, or rubbing, between her skis and the snow, slows her down. To fight friction, she puts wax on the bottom of her skis before the jump. This reduces friction. Less friction means more speed. And more speed means a better jump.

As Lindsey speeds down the hill, she has to push against the force of the air. That slows her down.

To fight this, Lindsey reduces air resistance by changing the shape of her body. She bends her knees and puts her arms behind her. That way there isn't as much air to push out of the way. Think about the shape of a sports car. Its shape keeps a lot of air from pushing against it. It's the same for Lindsey when she tucks down.

More Force = More Speed

Newton's second law of motion says that mass affects how an object accelerates. A smaller person generates a smaller force. That could mean less acceleration. So Lindsey's mass affects how fast she skis down the hill.

4. Landing

The Crucial Leap

Lindsey skis down the in-run for only a few seconds before the take off.

She must position her body and her skis at just the right angle as she leaps. She must quickly jump upward and outward at just the right moment. If she jumps a moment too late, she'll have to balance herself. That will result in a shorter jump. If she springs too early, she could fall down the hill.

Newton's Three Laws of Motion

Newton figured out how all objects move. The ideas in his laws of motion describe the forces that happen during a ski jump.

First Law of Motion: A moving object keeps moving at the same speed and in the same direction unless a force acts on it. A resting object will stay at rest unless a force acts on it.

Second Law of Motion: The power of the force and an object's mass affect how the object accelerates.

Third Law of Motion: For every action, there is an equal and opposite reaction.

Sweet Victory. Lindsey celebrates after her winning jump at the 2009 World Championships.

Need a Lift?

Because Lindsey angles her body and her skis just right, she "catches the air." This means she positions her body so that the air pushes against her. This acts against gravity and slows her return to the ground. When Lindsey catches the air, she gets **lift.** Lift helps objects stay in the air.

Newton's third law of motion helps explain how lift works. The third law states that for every action, there is an equal and opposite reaction.

A bird flying in the air is an example of lift. The bird flaps its wings down. That's the action. The reaction is the air pushing the bird up.

As Lindsey soars through the air, her body and skis push air downward. That's the action. In turn, the air actually pushes Lindsey up. That's the reaction.

Lindsey's V-shape position creates a bigger surface area below her body. She's able to push more air down. In reaction, more air pushes her up, giving her a boost.

A Happy Landing

As she descends from the jump, Lindsey's skis touch back down on the snow. What force pulls Lindsey back down to Earth?

You guessed it—gravity. This is another example of Newton's first law of motion. Gravity is the force that acts on Lindsey. It keeps her from soaring forever.

As Lindsey lands, she knows she jumped far. In fact, she jumped 97.5 meters (about 320 feet). That's even longer than the length of a football field!

Finally, the edges of Lindsey's skis run into the snow. This increases the friction between her skis and the snow. This slows her down and she comes to a stop. Now it's time to celebrate!

Olympic Dreams

Olympic Dreams

Lindsey Van began ski jumping when she was just 7 years old. Since then, she has dreamed of winning an Olympic gold medal.

Ski jumping started at the first Winter Olympics in 1924. But women have never been allowed to compete.

In 2009, the International Olympic Committee said that women's ski jumping was still not ready to be a part of the Winter Olympics. They said there were not enough women ski jumpers around the world.

But women ski jumpers disagreed. They knew of 80 women ski jumpers from 14 countries who could participate.

These women felt it was not fair. After all, men and women use exactly the same technique during a ski jump.

The only difference is women need to gain a bit more speed to jump the same distances as men. That's because women are usually lighter than men.

Even with this difference, Lindsey has jumped farther than men. In fact, she held the record for the longest jump—men or women—on Whistler Olympic Park Hill in 2008.

Hope for the Future

Lindsey and her fellow ski jumpers have hope. They believe that the Olympics will someday let women jump.

The sport is growing. Hundreds of young girls are learning to ski jump.

So, when the next Winter Olympics rolls around, tune in. Hopefully, you'll see the U.S. Women's Ski Jumping Team winning Olympic gold.

Wordwise

force: a push or pull

friction: a force that slows down the motion of an object that is touching something else as it moves

lift: a force that helps objects stay in the air

Laws at Play

Newton's laws of motion don't just happen on a ski jump. Motion is everywhere. Forces are acting on you all the time.

You can feel forces push against you when you ride your bike against the wind. You can feel friction when you run and stop on a gym floor. And gravity is pulling on you right now, keeping you on the Earth's surface.

You can notice the laws of motion anywhere you go. Think about a playground. From running around to the merry-go-round, the laws of motion are at play.

Stop Fast

You can find the first law of motion in action during a race. A girl is racing her friends. She's an object in motion! She tries to stop fast. But she doesn't stop right away. She moves forward a little as she steadies herself.

That's Newton's first law. It says a moving object tends to keep moving unless a force acts on it.

An object at rest stays at rest unless a force acts on it.

The more mass an object has, the harder it is for it to increase speed.

Push Me, Please!

Newton's first law also says that an object at rest stays at rest unless a force acts on it.

A small child sits in a swing, waiting for someone to push her. She's not going anywhere until someone gives her a push. She is staying at rest until another force acts upon her.

Faster, Higher!

Finally, the child's mother gives her a gentle push. But she wants to go higher. So her mother uses more force. She gives her a bigger push. Now she's swinging faster and higher.

That's Newton's second law in action. It says a greater force makes an object accelerate more.

Heads Up

Imagine that you're playing catch. Your friend throws the ball and you catch it. You use force to stop it. That's an easy force to see.

But sometimes you can't see the forces acting on a moving object. Let's say your friend throws the ball way over your head. You jump to catch the ball, but it's too high.

Newton's first law says that a moving object keeps moving at the same speed and in the same direction unless a force acts on it. So does the ball keep going up into the sky? No. Gravity is the force that pulls it back down to Earth. When it lands, it rolls on the ground. Do you have to chase it forever? No. Friction is the force that slows it down, and it stops.

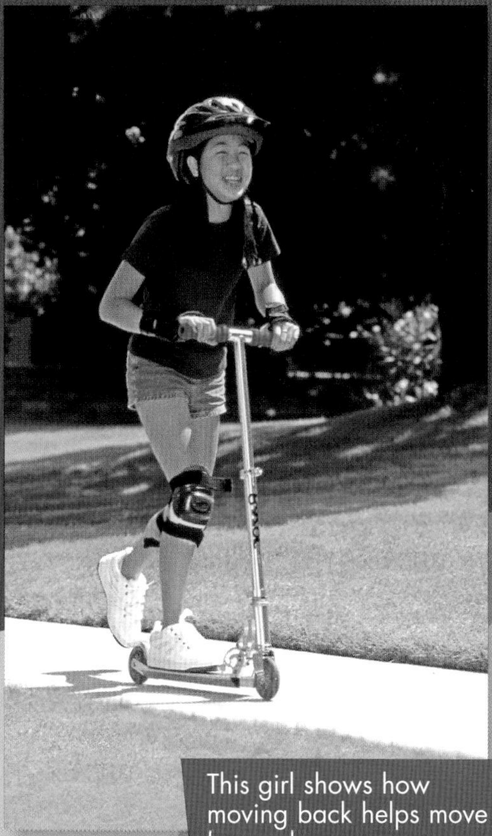

This girl shows how moving back helps move forward.

Push Back, Go Forward

Newton's third law states that for every action, there is an equal and opposite reaction.

Sometimes you can see this law in action. Think of kids riding their scooters. To move forward, they push one foot back.

You can also see it back by the swings. To get going, kids push their feet forward on the ground. In turn, they move backward.

Most of the time, you can't see the third law in action. But it's happening.

Think about any time you jump. As you jump, your foot pushes against the ground. In turn, the ground pushes back. It's true! If the ground didn't push back, your foot would crash through the ground.

Everyday Science

Forces are always acting on you, whether you are playing sports, having fun at the playground, or reading a book.

So the next time you go to the playground, think like a scientist. See if you can spot the laws of motion in action.

Laws of Motion

Ready, Set, Go! Let's find out how much you learned about forces and the laws of motion.

1. Name two forces that slow Lindsey down as she skis down the hill.

2. What force pulls objects down to Earth?

3. Which force helps Lindsey stay in the air after she jumps?

4. Which of Newton's laws explains why ski jumpers can't stay in the air forever?

5. According to Newton's second law, what do you need to do to throw a ball farther?